Learn to Stress

Less

50 simple and effective tips for a
stress-free life plus 2 bonus tips for
Christmas and New Year

Dr Vee Freir

ISBN: 1530927382
ISBN-13: 978-1530927388

DEDICATION

For my wonderful sons Finlay and Dougal Freir

ACKNOWLEDGEMENTS

I'd like to thank all my followers on Twitter, without whom this book would never have even been started and all those at Self-Publishing School, who enabled me to take it to the finish line. I'd also like to thank my editor, Russell Turner from Bassman Books, for doing yet another sterling job, and all those who read my book prior to launch and gave me much-needed feedback. Thanks guys!

Website: www.dr-vee.co.uk
Twitter: @dr_vee11

This book is not intended to take the place of medical advice. If you are experiencing stress and are in any doubt, please contact your **GP** or a Health Professional

FOREWORD

As a management consultant I often come into contact with overstressed people and, although what I can offer may relieve stressful situations, I have observed that it provides only temporary relief for stressed individuals, as something else invariably comes along to wind them up again. I have often wished I could do more to help them cope with the inevitable roller coaster ride that seems to be a necessary part of our business and personal lives.

Now, in this small book I have discovered a tool kit of practical, easy to use tips that will work for every individual and every situation. Keep it handy and when you start to feel stressed simply scan the headings until you find the tip that's right for you and follow it.

Before long you will find your favourites and after a while you won't need to refer to the book so often. With practice you will have made the tips part of your everyday life, to the benefit of your health and happiness and the joy of those around you.

Stress less and live more.

Jim McGuire B.Sc, C. Eng. MBA
Principal Consultant,
Methodology - Methods and Technology for Business Performance

INTRODUCTION

Stress is one of the biggest problems in today's world and it affects all of us from time to time.

Do you ever find yourself wanting a quick way to relax or to let go of your stressed feelings?

Well, this book is full of helpful, tried and trusted tips for you to try. They have been used by many people and I can tell you I have 'road tested' every single one myself, so I know they work.

As a Consultant Clinical Psychologist who has seen many people suffer from stress-related problems and has also, because I'm human too, had my own moments of stress to deal with, I'm always looking for ways to help myself and others let go of stress.

A few years ago I wrote a five-step book on dealing with stress called 'START to Stress Less'. People found it helpful, so I added to that concept by writing a weekly tip on Twitter for people to try out. They seemed to work well in the 140 character format, but of course it did not give people the 'why this tip works', just the tip itself. I've had quite a few Twitter followers ask if I could put those tips into a simple format, explaining the how and why they work, so that they have all the tips in one place and so the idea of this book came about. Choosing just 50 tips out of all the ones I have written was the biggest stress of all!

Trying out these tips on a weekly basis gave my

followers something to work with. More than that, it also let them see that there is never just one solution, there are lots of ways to quickly and simply deal with stress. They could become creative with their solutions and build up an arsenal of ways to manage different situations.

Many of my followers on Twitter have messaged me to say how helpful they have found certain tips, but the thing is, different people seem to prefer different ones. That is why this book has lots of different ideas, so you can find out which ones specifically work for you and in which situations, though I have to say that if you do all 50 you will probably find, like I do, that they become part of a tool-kit to keep you feeling good and not worried about life's stresses at all, because you always know you have something quick to implement that will help.

I promise that if you try each tip, it will become very clear very quickly which ones are your favourites, though I can assure you each one works on its own, but who doesn't want choice? And after you've tried all 50 you can see it as being part of a mental health first aid box. When you have a cut, you reach for a plaster don't you? And you reach for one the right size to fit the situation. So here, if you find yourself feeling stressy, you reach for your stress tip tools and see which one fits the bill. No more getting caught up in your stressed feelings, just a simple way to deal with it.

So don't delay. Get started today and see how much just using the first tip can help you feel a sense of calm and control over your life. And if that is what the first tip can do, think how you will feel after you have tried all 50 tips.

Take control of your stress and don't let it control you.

A simple idea and in this simple book you will learn how you can change your life for the better.

BEFORE I START, A WORD ABOUT BREATHING....

Everyone talks about taking a breath and how much breathing helps when you feel stressed, so I'm not even going to put this as one of my tips, even if it is one of the major things that will help combat rising feelings of stress when they come.

Instead I'm going to give you, right here, right now the 'how to breathe' that I wrote in my book 'START to Stress Less' because I feel that it's instrumental to know how to breathe to feel the benefits. And quite a few of my tips do contain the message that you need to take a breath.

When we become stressed we very often breathe shorter and faster. This is designed to get us into action – the 'fight/flight response', which I don't want to go into in detail here because I want to get to the nitty gritty of breathing well. If you want to know more then please read my book 'START to Stress Less' where you'll find out all you need to know.

So here it is:

'In order for your body to start the correct method to get into fight/flight, your body needs as much oxygen as possible to get your muscles working. Your muscles need to tense, so that you can either fight or run away. Your heart needs to beat faster to pump that blood round and round your body. You need to breathe in a certain way in order to get that oxygen into your body quickly. What happens is that your breathing becomes

shorter and faster. You will probably not realise this is what you do, unless you spend a little time becoming aware.

One of the best ways to start recognising what your breathing is like, is to watch yourself in a mirror. If you can, do this now. If not, then do remember to try this when you can, as it is absolutely vital that you know what your body is doing.

So, I am going to assume that you have time now. Stand in front of a mirror (the best mirror for this purpose is one where you can see the whole of your upper body). As you are standing in front of the mirror, take a few deep breaths and watch your chest.

What do you notice? Do your shoulders go up as you breathe in and your shoulders go down as you breathe out? If this is what you see when you breathe, then this is a perfect example of nice, shallow breathing. Not deep breathing at all!

Now for a bit of a physiology lesson, albeit in very simple terms. In your abdomen is a slab of muscle called the diaphragm which is kind of dome shaped. Above the diaphragm sit your lungs and below sit your other organs such as your stomach and liver. When you breathe deeply, what should happen is your diaphragm goes down, creating space for your lungs to expand. So, if you are breathing deeply, what you should see is your belly going out as you breathe in, and then in when you breathe out. Your shoulders should not move at all.

A very good example of good, deep breathing can be seen if you watch a baby. Watch their tummy and see what happens when they are asleep. Another good example is to watch a dog or a cat when they are relaxing.

Now try this. Place your hands on your tummy, with the finger tips of each hand touching the finger tips of the other hand. As you breathe in, see if you can get your tummy to expand, and watch what happens to your fingers. They should part slightly. An easier way to do this is to lie on the floor, placing your hands in the same way as before, and see if you can get your fingers to part slightly as you breathe in, by letting your tummy expand.

If you find this difficult, close your eyes and as you breathe in, think of your lungs expanding as you breathe in, and deflating as you breathe out. Imagine, as you breathe in, filling up your lungs from the bottom, right up to the top. And then as you breathe out, you empty your lungs from the top, all the way down to the bottom, allowing your diaphragm to push all the air out. This can take a bit of practice to get right.

Another way is to put your hands on your sides and feel your ribs moving as you breathe in and out. Again think about your lungs expanding as your ribs move out, and then contracting as your ribs move in.

Now try to make your outbreath longer than your inbreath. A good way to do this is to do the following: As you breathe in count to two, and as you breathe out count to three or four. Try it like this: In, one, two. Out, one, two, three. You might need to play with this a bit and experiment with breathing in for three and out for four, or in for four and out for five and so on, until you find a level that is comfortable for you. But remember, always make the outbreath longer than the inbreath.

The reason for your outbreath to be longer than your inbreath is because when we are stressed we tend to make our outbreath very short. Therefore doing the opposite gets the relaxation response going, and the relaxation response is the reverse of the stress response.

The great thing about breathing is that if you want to have a different body response, you just have to change your breathing pattern. Your breathing can either calm your body down or get it ready for the fight/flight response. That is the power of the breath.'

I hope this has explained how you can change how you breathe to enable you to manage when you feel stressed. So, whenever I mention the word 'breathe' in this tip book, please remember what it is I'm talking about.

Onward to the tips!

TIP 1

On waking take a minute or two to notice your whole body lying on the bed before getting up.

Why:
Very often when we wake up in the morning the first thing we do is think about what we're doing or that we want something right now e.g. a cup of coffee, a longer lie-in. We're based in our thinking at that moment. But in order to stop ourselves getting carried away with thinking – because the very next thing on the 'thought list' will be something along the lines of 'what am I doing today' or thinking about all the things we've got on the agenda – if we come into our body and do a very quick body scan (don't worry, I'll explain that below), see which muscles are tense and just have the word 'relax' in our minds, then we can come out of our thinking grounded in the moment and it gives us a chance to start our day feeling calm. And what a great way to start the day!

A body scan is where we literally scan our bodies from head to toe (or the other way about, it doesn't matter).

By holding the word 'relax' in our minds, we're effectively giving our body a clue as to what we want. Give this a try: hold your arm out in front of you and say the word 'tense' in your mind. Do you notice a slight tension in your arm? Now, say the word 'relax' in your mind. See the difference? It might only be a slight difference, but that's the difference that can make the difference. Seriously.

Okay, I hear you say, but what if I need to go to the toilet in a rush? Well, it happens to all of us! In this scenario, please, rush out of bed and get to the toilet, but once you've done what you need to do, just sit on the toilet and do the body scan. It works just as well sitting as lying down.

And if you forget to do it very first thing, while you are waiting for the kettle to boil, do the body scan standing up.

Calm start to the day, that is what you are aiming for.

TIP 2

Overwhelmed by what's happening in the world? Don't forget you can always use the 'off' button.

Why:
It's good to be informed of all that is happening in the world. Keeping up to date with news is an important part of that. But have you ever thought about how much the news is geared to all the bad things happening and, in comparison, rarely the good or the lovely things that are going on?

Spend an evening watching the news. In just one programme probably 95% at least is devoted to all the negative and distressing things that are happening. Try it out. How do you feel as you watch all this awfulness happening? Does it make you feel good about yourself? Calm? Relaxed?

Secondly, think how many times in a day you read, listen to, or watch the news as it pours forth. If you are on Twitter, Facebook or any other social media site you should count those in too.

So here's the thing: Make an evaluation. Do you need to watch or listen more than once a day? If you do, well fine, but even so, how many times would suffice for you to realise that you are aware of what is happening in the world?

Once you have decided how much time you need to listen, stick to that. Whenever you are tempted to switch it on again remind yourself not to.

Remember, once you begin to feel tension in your body, you can always use that 'off' button.

TIP 3

Make sure your posture is upright and balanced.

Why:
We are not just a mind and not just a body, the two work together. And if one is out of balance you can be sure the other is. So, if your body is balanced then the chances are your mind can also be.

If you sit at a computer, check in with yourself. Are you hunched over? Chin on your chest? Looking down a lot, or up? Shoulders rounded or tense? And what about when you are sitting watching television or reading? What happens to your body then? Or do you sit with your legs crossed?

Take a pause and start by uncrossing your legs. Now see if you can lift your head from your crown (not the front of your head, the very tip of your head, which if you drew a line from the floor right up through your body, would actually be the top-most point on your scalp). Try thinking of a piece of thread that is fixed right through your body to the ceiling and feel yourself being pulled up by that thread. Can you notice your spine elongates?

Check that you are sitting square on the chair, which means that there is equal pressure on each buttock.

Allow your eyes to look ahead for a moment or two, relax your shoulders, let tension drain from your arms.

And what about if you are standing? Check that your feet are square on the floor, that is that you feel equal pressure on the ball of your foot and your heel… not so easy to do if you're wearing heels, but give it a go. You don't need to move much to get that sense of equal pressure on the floor, it's just a small movement. Soften your knees slightly. Check that your upper body isn't leaning forward or back. Nice and square. See if you can elongate your spine by doing the same exercise as in the paragraph above about sitting. Then allow your eyes to look ahead and relax shoulders and arms.

Body relaxed, mind can relax.

Notice that I said relaxed and not sunken. If you collapse your posture, this has as detrimental an effect as being too rigid.

So go on, at least once every day, if not more often, check in with your posture.

TIP 4

Set a timer to go off every hour and when it does take a moment to relax.

Why:

It is very easy to get caught up in whatever we are doing, whether that's sitting at a desk at work, looking after children or even if you are stuck in bed feeling ill. So setting a timer to go off every hour is a great way to remind yourself to take a moment and check in with your body to check for any areas of tension.

When you do this check-in, scan your body from either head to toe or toe to head and see if there are any points of tension. This literally should take seconds. If there are, just focus on the word 'relax' in your mind. The aim isn't to force yourself to relax, because all that will do is build tension, but if you focus on the word 'relax' your body will respond.

If you do not notice any tension anywhere in your body, it's worth focusing on the word 'relax' anyway as it certainly won't do you any harm.

TIP 5

Are your expectations realistic? Take time to check. If they are unrealistic, redefine them.

Why:
We often expect too much of ourselves and this can cause stress and tension in the body. Stress can manifest in so many different ways, from physical symptoms such as headaches and digestive disorders to chaotic thinking and anxiety and depression. So this week, every day, take a look at your expectations. Write them down if it helps, by making a list of your expectations and checking if they're realistic by asking yourself the question, 'Is this expectation realistic?' If it is... great. If it's not, rewrite it so that it becomes realistic.

It can be useful to do this both in the morning and at night: in the morning, so that you can set yourself up for the day knowing that you can achieve what you want to; last thing at night, so that you can have a restful night.

TIP 6

Feeling stressed? Exercise. No need for the gym, just get your body moving e.g. go for brisk walk.

Why:
Human beings are not designed to be sitting down and movement is essential for good body function. If your body isn't functioning well, then your mind can't either as the two are inexorably linked together. You really cannot separate your body and mind.

Exercise releases endorphins, sometimes called 'happy hormones', into the body, which is good in itself. They not only improve our mood but can help us to sleep better too.

Also, exercise allows us to focus on the movement and not on our thoughts or ruminations about feeling stressed.

And, if you are feeling bloated or suffer from constipation, moving can really help.

The good news is that when I say 'exercise' I don't mean going to the gym or doing hard exercise. Exercise in any form will do, unless going to the gym or running floats your boat! You can do yoga, some stretching, T'ai Chi or Qiqong or just go for a walk. A brisk walk is better than a slow one, but even a slow walk is better than none.

When people tell me they don't have any time to exercise, I always ask them to keep a diary of what they do do. It has, so far, 100% of the time proved that they have far more time than they thought. For instance, if you spend time sitting watching the television, then do yourself a favour and do five minutes of exercise before you sit down to watch. One of the things I encourage people to do is walk or run up and down the stairs several times before sitting down. That seems to do the trick.

However, please do go and see your GP if you haven't exercised for quite a while, just to get yourself checked out. This is especially important if you are overweight or underweight, recently had surgery or are recovering from an injury.

TIP 7

Got a list of things to be done? Make a new list with the first five items on your list and do them today.

Why:

I don't know about you, but I'm continually making lists just in case I forget something. Lists are great as they can be a good way to get things done, but at the end of each day, if you find yourself putting things from your today list onto tomorrow's, it can be undermining, as though there is just no end in sight.

So instead of repeating lists day in day out, if you make a new list with just the first five items on (you can make it three or four if you want) then make absolutely sure you complete those five today. As soon as you can.

Once you've achieved those five, how do you feel? That you've achieved something? Because you should. Give yourself a pat on the back.

Oh yes, and don't make a new list until tomorrow. You don't want to spoil your sense of achievement now do you?

TIP 8

Rushing first thing in the morning doesn't help stress levels. Try getting up just 10 minutes earlier.

Why:

If we start the day in a state of stress, the chances are that those stress levels will build during the day, but if we start by feeling that we've got everything in hand and we can be calm, then at the very least our day will start well.

I often hear people saying that they can't get up earlier, but they seem to think that when we're talking about earlier, we mean an hour or something like that. But if you make a commitment to get up just a few minutes earlier each day – start with just three minutes earlier, five minutes the next day, eight the one after that and ten on day four – then it hardly feels like you're changing much at all.

Small steps can go a long way to help us achieve those goals.

And when you get up ten minutes earlier in the day, believe me, you can fit in a whole lot more. In fact it's quite amazing what you can do in ten minutes. Here are some examples: a short meditation; some stretching exercises; yoga moves; reading a chapter of a self-help book; learning a few words of a foreign language; having a restful and quiet cup of tea. The list is endless.

When you get up ten minutes earlier you can literally change how you start your day and is so worth doing. Give it a try.

TIP 9

Feeling unconfident? Try changing the way you stand. A relaxed yet strong pose is what you're aiming for.

Why:

I just want to start by saying that confidence is situational. For instance, are you confident that you can make a cup of your favourite beverage? Of course you are! Because you don't even think about this at all. So what other things can the confident you do? You might not feel confident talking to new people, but I bet you're confident talking to your friends? Am I right? So this means that you have confidence when you know something or know how to do something. This means you are confident, just not all the time. And this is important. We often think and talk ourselves into our feelings and most often those are negative and impact on us hugely. We tell ourselves we can't.

Well, confident people, or those who appear confident – because no-one is confident in every single situation they find themselves in, even those who appear confident have their moments when they're not feeling it – focus on what they can control. The one thing we can all control is our body language, as long as we think about it and change it accordingly.

It has been shown by Amy Cuddy, a Professor at Harvard Business School, that just by taking up what she calls 'power poses' can change the way you feel in any situation. And the beauty of it is, it's simple! She advocates practising for a couple of minutes first thing in the morning, but I'd say yes, by all means do that, but practise whenever you can right throughout the day.

And one great way to discover what pose you should adopt is to copy someone who you think is confident and mirror the way they stand.

The kind of pose you're aiming for is one where you're standing square on your feet, head up with the crown of your head towards the ceiling, eyes facing straight ahead, shoulders relaxed, and see if you can think of your core (that place right in the very middle of your body) and lift up from there. Now think 'relaxed and confident' while you stand like this.

You will need to practise if you're not used to standing like this. Once you've got the standing down to a fine art, see if you can do the same while sitting and then walking.

Cuddy A (2015) Presence: Bringing your boldest self to your biggest challenges. Little, Brown & Co.

TIP 10

Instead of big changes, try making small ones. Just 1% difference accumulates if you keep it up.

Why:

Whenever we want to make changes in our lives it's funny how we always go for the big things. And it makes it hard for us to achieve what we want or we give up really quickly because it's just too much to ask.

There's this great story about Dave Brailsford, who took on the role of Performance Director of the UK Olympic cycling team in 2003. He looked at each and every cyclist and their machines and changed everything by just 1%. And of course the rest is history, as they say, with Team GB cyclists becoming the envy of the world.

Well, if we put this principle into the way we change things then it can reap big rewards.

Here's an example: I want to get fitter and I don't like going to the gym (I don't, really I don't!) and the very thought of spending more than a few minutes every day exercising makes me break out in a sweat. Instead, every time I go up and down the stairs (and in my house I have fifteen stairs) I go up and down once more each time (so I run up and down twice instead of once). That is a small change but will accumulate into a big difference. I'm talking one flight of stairs here by the way, not the Empire State Building!

Or here's another one: taking a minute in every hour to think about relaxing every muscle in your body.

Change doesn't have to be big to make a change!

TIP 11

Focus on what you have in your life, not on what's lacking.

Why:

When we focus on what we want it can add to our feelings of inadequacy or deprivation and that can add significantly to our stress levels. It keeps reminding us that we are not good enough, need more things to make us happy, and on and on it goes.

By focusing on what we have it can let us see that our lives are all right and we have a lot to be grateful for.

Of course, there are always things that we might want, for instance a job if we don't have one, but instead of that, think of all the positive attributes you could bring to a job. Write them down. Now check your CV, does it reflect all that you're capable of?

Or what if, by comparing yourself to others, you think you don't have enough friends? Well what about the friends you do have? It's often said in these times of the social media boom that we can feel inadequate next to our friends who maybe have thousands of Facebook friends, but how many of those are real friends? And I'm talking someone you can phone in the middle of the night because you need them? Not many, I'm guessing! But that's the thing… we have very few real friends compared to acquaintances. Do you see what I'm getting at here?

So, look at what you have and focus on that.

TIP 12

**Chin sticking out = adds to feelings of stress.
Level chin = lessens feelings of stress.**

Why:
One of the things that can really help to lessen our feelings of stress, as pointed out at the very beginning of this book, is to breathe properly. Diaphragmatic breathing. Go ahead and go back and reacquaint yourself with that concept if you've forgotten.

Well, if you stick your chin out, it stops that smooth flow of breath and shortens it, which can set the body into automatic pilot for feeling anxious and stressed. While I'm on the subject, if you constantly walk about with your chin down, you're also closing off the airway to support a good breath. Often people who spend their lives looking down can feel low and anxious at the same time. Interesting when you see so many people on their mobile phones looking down, don't you think?

So the best way to allow a good breath to flow is to have your chin level. It takes a bit of practice, and looking in the mirror to check on yourself, but it really works. And the beauty of it is that it's not usually much of a change. The way to do it is to think of the very crown of your head and tilt that towards the ceiling. It's not a big movement.

I teach Qiqong, a slow martial art form similar to T'ai Chi, and I'm always on the lookout for a sticking out chin or one that's pointing down. When I alter the way people hold their heads by either a small movement up or down of the chin, they are amazed at how different it can feel.

It can help if you have someone you trust look at you and set your chin level for you to start with, as you learn to hold yourself differently.

And remember in Tip 10 that I was talking about small change accumulating to big change. And this is one of those appearing to be small things that can really help to keep us calm and collected in all situations.

TIP 13

When coming back from work and before entering your house, take a few breaths and let go of the day.

Why:
When we carry our work into our home, no matter whether we have family waiting there for us or live alone, all that it does is add to our stress levels. But letting go of our work life and delineating the boundary between work and home can really help us to relax once we get through our front door.

We have to remember that work is work and home is home. Yes, we might well have to take some work home with us, but we need a bit of respite between the work/home scenarios.

If you have a family to come home to it's even more important to let go of your work. They might want to know how your day has gone and that's fine, but if you take everything that's happened during the day and keep repeating it – and let's face it we usually tell people the awful things that have happened rather than the good bits – we're actually re-enacting those scenarios to some degree. I always talk about memories as echoes.

Try this: think of something that happened yesterday, it can be good or bad, and as you think about it can you feel your body beginning to react to the memory? Interestingly we can't have a thought without a body sensation or an emotion attached to it, even if it's a neutral thought. Memories are scenarios that our mind brings up for us in the form of thoughts, physical sensations and/or emotions. So the moment we think about something that happened, we're already there... back in it so to speak, even if it's only slightly. Or as I said, an echo.

If we take a moment before entering the home to take a breath or two (and you can remind yourself about breathing by going to the very beginning of the book) and tell ourselves, we are home now, we can let go of the work day and begin our home part of the day, we have a great opportunity to enter the house calmly.

And entering the house calmly will allow you to let go of feelings of stress so much more easily and at least start this part of the day by being relaxed.

TIP 14

Think you know? Take a pause and open yourself to what else is out there. You might surprise yourself.

Why:
One of the intriguing things is that everything, yes everything, changes. But we don't often notice it.

Scientists spend their lives creating theories and proving that they are right, then the next moment someone comes along and disproves that theory and tells us something new.

When we shut ourselves off from the fact that there is far more out there to know than we can ever imagine, it leads to stagnation, rigid thinking and a whole lot more. And when I say 'rigid', think about that word for a second and see what it does to your body.

Our minds and our bodies are inexorably linked, so we can't think of something like rigidity or being closed off without having some kind of sense in our bodies what that means.

Have you ever spoken to someone who is so convinced that they are right that they will argue their case and get hyped up over the thought that they are the only ones who know or are right? How difficult is that person to deal with? Are they tense as they argue their case?

So what I'm trying to say here is that rigidity in any

form adds to our feelings of rigidity in the body and that leads to feelings of tightness and stress. And one way of counteracting that – and we can only deal with ourselves here – is to remind ourselves that there are many solutions and many things that we don't know. When we open ourselves to that thought, not only do we become more creative, we also stop tensing and give ourselves an opportunity to relax and can let go of stressful bodily feelings.

TIP 15

Feeling tense? Focus on relaxing your hands first. Then relax the rest of your body.

Why:
Our hands are a real giveaway. It's the very first thing I look at when I see a client. What are their hands doing? It tells me so much. And I have to say it's a rare thing for me to meet a client for the first time whose hands are relaxed. Why? Well coming to see a psychologist for the first time is a stressful thing!

If I'm working on relaxation with someone, I will often ask them to soften their hands first and see what difference that makes. It's hard to be anxious and stressed if your hands are loose and relaxed. Really it is!

So go on – think of something stressful right now. It doesn't have to be a big thing, just something small and simple and notice your hands. Now, focus on relaxing your hands. Soften them. I use words like 'soften' and 'flow', so focus on those words and see what happens. Now as you focus on your hands being soft and relaxed try thinking of that stressful thing again. See the difference?

Where this can really help is when you are driving. As you drive notice your hands on the steering wheel and see if you can soften them a touch. Just enough so that you're still in control of the steering wheel. Once your hands are soft enough, think about your arms and your shoulders. Now soften them. Hopefully by now you'll notice that you're not holding yourself rigidly. This is important when driving because if anything happens, if you're rigid then it's not easy to be flexible. But if you're relaxed you can be flexible. Relaxed, flexible body leads to a relaxed, flexible mind. And flexible thinking can go a long way to keep you alert and able to negotiate the car well when you have to react to suddenly.

Another scenario is when you're about to go into a meeting with someone who you find a bit difficult. Before you go in to the room, notice your hands and take a second or two to soften them, then your arms and then your shoulders. And then take a breath and enter the room. When you enter calmly it can make such a difference to your interactions. It can be quite a good thing to practise this with people you don't find stressful first and then use it in stressful situations. Practice makes perfect.

TIP 16

Random acts of kindness can bring joy to both the giver and the receiver. Try to do at least one each day this week.

Why:

Whenever we are feeling stressed the tendency is to be quite self-absorbed. As in noticing everything that is wrong with our lives and our very being. We notice more aches and pains, thoughts about our adequacy can border on the obsessive, as can thinking about what we can do to make things better. On and on it goes.

If we stop for a moment and start to think about others, what happens? We have to come out of ourselves and our focus starts to broaden. We are already thinking about something else, which is a great start.

There have been quite a few studies on this and one, by Raposa and colleagues, suggests that doing things for others that come from an attitude of kindness within ourselves can help boost our positive emotions, cope with stress and improve our mental health.

What I would like to say here though is that an act of kindness does not have to be something big, or spectacular. Being kind can be something as simple as smiling at someone, or putting a coin into a collection box.

Of course there are many larger gestures that we may want to make for those we love or for those who we feel may need a boost in their lives.

It doesn't really matter what you choose to do, but see if you can manage to do one kind thing for someone else every single day this week and see how it makes you feel.

Raposa EB, Laws HB, Ansell EB (2015) Prosocial Behavior Mitigates the Negative Effects of Stress in Everyday Life. Clinical Psychology Science December 10, 2015

TIP 17

Get away from blame. Focus on what your needs are and what you can do to make things better for yourself and others.

Why:

When we focus on blame, we are already in a negative mindset. We're looking for someone to point a finger at, so they can be responsible. How do you think this impacts on ourselves? Well, if we're in a negative mindset, looking for others to blame, we're already tight and closed off. And that means on the stress pathway. It also focuses on what's wrong.

So, the next time you want to blame someone for something, change the focus. What are your needs in this situation? What could you do, right now, to make things better? That's your responsibility and is totally within your power to do something about.

By taking this open stance it makes us more open and positive thinking. And it also offers a great opportunity for creativity.

Another way to think about this is that blaming someone for something that has already happened does not help fix it. It just keeps whatever it is and the people involved stuck in the past and feeling bad about themselves.

For sure, it can help people to know where they've gone wrong and, in some ways, that could be construed as good. But do you think that people might already have an idea of what they did? If they genuinely don't recognise it, then I think it is okay to point out that mistakes were made, but focusing on how things could be put right, or changed so that the same mistakes don't happen again, can foster an attitude of cohesive working and creative thinking. And above all it is very good team management.

Blame shuts us down and creates negativity. Focusing on what could be done in this situation opens us up, creates positivity and makes us be more creative. The choice is yours!

TIP 18

Does your jaw feel tight? Take a deep breath, open your mouth slightly and as you exhale say 'ahhh'.

Why:
We can hold a lot of stress in our jaw and we can feel it most often as a tightness just at the corner of our jawbone, under our ears. When we collect stress here it can lead to all sorts of discomfort from a minor ache to full on toothache or headache.

To relax our jaw we need to do something. Massaging the area can help a little, but this can be painful, especially if there's lots of tension. So this way of releasing the jaw can really help to alleviate any discomfort that may have built up.

Whenever I do this I do it several times and then make sure my lips are slightly apart at the end so that my jawbone can slacken off.

There's no problem at all with doing this several times a day and it can be a very effective thing to do last thing at night, as there's nothing better than going to bed having a relaxed jaw.

TIP 19

Stop right now and think of all the things you're grateful for. Do this at least once per day.

Why:

If someone has been grateful to you for something, how does it make you feel? Good, right? And guess what? Gratitude works both ways. It's hard to feel negative and stressed when someone is being kind and telling us they are grateful for something. The same goes when we are offering gratitude.

Being grateful allows us to detach ourselves from our negative thinking, creates a sense of well-being and puts the focus on the positive. And when we focus on the positive, there is a sense of feeling good that arises and that can cut through negative thoughts or feelings. So gratitude turns us from inward thinking – about ourselves, to outward thinking – about others.

Also, if you think about it, when we perform a simple act of gratitude, like saying 'thank you' to someone, it fosters a connection with another being, which not only shows us in a good light, but can increase our sense of belonging. And it can even win us new friends.

The good news is that there is a wealth of research out there to back this up. Robert Emmons, Professor of Psychology at University of California, a world leading authority in the field of gratitude and its pay-offs, suggests it can help everything from feeling less stressed to sleeping better and has both physical and mental benefits.

Being grateful can be a simple thing of saying 'thank you' to anyone who has done something for us, for example people at the check-out in a shop, or a waitress/waiter in a coffee shop. Or we can thank the people in our lives when they do something, like cook a meal or get us something that we need. Or we can just sit and focus on all we have that we are grateful for.

I'm sure you can think of loads of situations where you can show gratitude or think of things that you're thankful for in your life.

So go on – every single day this week make sure that you show gratitude. Small or big, it doesn't matter. What matters is that you do it!

Emmons RA (2013) Gratitude Works: A 21-day program for creating emotional prosperity. Jossey-Bass

TIP 20

Self-limiting beliefs exist only in your mind. Remind yourself of that when you find yourself listening to them.

Why:
Self-limiting beliefs are not truths, they're just thoughts that we create and believe. But they are insidious and we so often listen to the negative messages we give ourselves.

Beliefs are things that we convince ourselves are absolute truths. But this is what I say to people when they tell me something is absolutely true: we only know what we know until we know something different.

Let me give you an example: it wasn't so long ago that everyone thought the world was flat. Can you imagine sitting in your bed with the total belief that the world is flat and someone comes rushing in and says, 'Hey, guess what? The world is round!' Of course, you don't believe it because you're absolutely sure that the world is flat. But then it's proven without a doubt that the world is in fact round. Now what happens to your belief that the world is flat? It changes!

A self-limiting belief is only true if you believe it so. The next time you hear yourself talking to yourself about all the things that you can't do or you're limited to, remind yourself that it might be totally different. And if it is totally different, then it doesn't have to be self-limiting! Or as Henry Ford said, 'If you think you can do a thing or can't do a thing, you're right.'

It can be really fun to challenge our thinking, so go ahead. Give it a go. And see that the only person holding you back, most often, is yourself.

TIP 21

Shoulders tight? Imagine carrying a heavy rucksack. Imagine taking it off. Feel your shoulders relax.

Why:

There are points in the body where we tend to carry more stress than in others and the shoulders are one of them. When we feel stressed we can feel our shoulders tighten and scrunch up and if we stay like that it can mean all kinds of problems from headaches to sore neck just to name a couple of physical things. But the main problem is that, as I've explained before, tightness in the body most probably means tightness in the mind. And when our minds are tight, releasing stress becomes even harder.

This tip is such a simple one and yet it is so effective. The way to do it best is to close your eyes and imagine a really heavy rucksack on your back. Really sense its weight. It can be useful to think of a rucksack full of heavy rocks… that one always seems to work for me!

If you can visualise its colour, so much the better. If you're not good at visualisation it doesn't matter, go for a sense of what it might feel like.

The clearer a picture or sense of feeling you can get the better it will be, because what you're trying to do is create a complete sensory experience. That way you'll feel the benefit from what you do next.

Now, imagine taking that rucksack off. Imagine it either slipping off your shoulders or someone taking it off for you, whatever works best.

Let your shoulders fully relax now they don't have to carry around such a weight. Allow your neck to stretch up slightly and your arms stretch down. And breathe.

That should make a difference.

TIP 22

Monotask instead of multitask. Multitasking doubles the amount of time to do a task and at least doubles the mistakes.

Why:

According to MIT Neuroscientist Earl Miller, our brains are 'not wired to multitask well... when people think they're multitasking, they're actually just switching from one task to another very rapidly. And every time they do there's cognitive cost.'

So think about it. If all you're doing is switching from one task to another, albeit very rapidly, you can see that your focus of attention won't be on finishing one task. If instead you change things round and determine that you will finish one thing at a time, concentrating on that and not getting deflected by other things, you can finish one thing and then move on to the next with ease and without feeling overloaded.

Monotasking improves efficiency and quality of our work. That's because multitasking might feel like we're accomplishing a lot, but what's really happening is our brains get flooded with too much information, which slows us down and it becomes difficult to organise our thoughts well and filter out irrelevant information. And it will probably take longer to finish something when we're jumping back and forward from one thing to another

And of course, if we're flicking from one thing to

another, the chance of making mistakes is far larger.

There's an incredibly interesting study conducted at Stanford University – well okay, I found it interesting – but the outcome was that people who are high multitaskers were found to be constantly distracted and couldn't focus, which means that they were in real danger of brain overload. And brain overload leads to stress.

So the next time you sit down to email, just email. The moment you start to do something else, like watch TV too, you'll be overloading your brain.

Here's a great Roman Proverb I found: A man who chases two rabbits catches none. Worth remembering, I think.

Be Goals (2015) The Science of Multitasking
http://begoals.com/gtd/the-science-multitasking-vs-monotasking/

TIP 23

Notice 'What ifs' and stop them in their tracks. Practise focusing on the here and now.

Why:

Whenever we get stuck in a loop of telling ourselves 'What if...' all we're doing is focusing on the future. We don't know what is going to happen in the future, but we do know what is happening right now.

Focusing on the future can add to our stress levels as we conjure up pictures in our minds about all kinds of scenarios. Thoughts, physical sensations and emotional feelings are all inextricably linked. We actually can't have one without having the other two as well. So as we conjure up a future in our minds that doesn't exist yet, we're also creating emotional and physical sensations too. And sadly those can be all too real!

If you start thinking negatively, then your body will tighten and that can lead to stressful emotions and those in turn will activate more stressful thoughts and on and on it goes.

Okay, I hear you say, what about positive thoughts about an imagined future? I challenge you to see how many times you say 'What if' to yourself and have it be a positive thing? I doubt it's very often.

So I'm not talking about when we actively create a positive image of the future to help ourselves to do something, like give a speech for example. That can help. I'm talking about the incessant talking to ourselves of 'What if this happens, or that happens.'

When you find yourself in 'What if' mode this week, stop right there and say to yourself, 'What's happening right now?' See if you can feel your feet on the ground, look around and see what's around you and notice your breathing. Then carry on with whatever you're doing.

By learning to stop ourselves when we're in 'What if' mode we are teaching ourselves to get into the habit of changing the thinking, which leads to calming ourselves down. A very useful tool.

TIP 24

Start clearing out clutter. Start small. One tidied drawer will empower you.

Why:

When we live in a cluttered environment it can add hugely to our stress levels, from simple things like feeling embarrassed if someone calls round unexpectedly or just a general feeling of disorganisation, to not being able to locate the things we need immediately, such as important papers, or leading to feelings of being totally overwhelmed. And I'm sure you can think of many more.

So clutter is really another overload situation.

But the thing is, instead of starting by thinking you've got to do the whole lot in one go, try just doing one drawer. See how that makes you feel.

I have a great example from my own life. I admit I'm not the tidiest of people and I've always tended to just shove my knickers and socks in a drawer without much thought about it. But the drawer was hard to close. Well, one day I was in a bookshop and picked up a book on tidying and there were explicit pictures about how to fold knickers and socks, so instead of lying flat you roll them and stack them side by side. Okay, I thought. Worth a try. When I got home I opened my drawer and true to form, things just looked like they'd exploded. I took everything out and folded each item according to the explanation in the book and, lo and behold, I had more room in my drawer than I ever imagined. The drawer looked wonderful and I felt fantastic – so much so, that I couldn't help but keep opening it to see how great it looked!

I want to emphasise here that it's not so much about the actual folding or how you go about this, but the fact that one drawer tidied made me feel so good, and guess what happened next? Yes, I went on to do all my drawers the same way. I also got bags of all the stuff that was cluttering my closet and gave them away to the charity shop, which also made me feel very good. And I've not had an 'exploding' drawer since. I learned my lesson.

So go on… what's stopping you? Get one drawer tidied, no matter if it's a kitchen drawer, a desk drawer or a knicker drawer. Just do it and see how it makes you feel. Clear out all the things you haven't used in years… because let's face it, if you haven't used them in years, you're unlikely to start doing so. They're just things taking up space in your life.

And things that take up space in our lives also take up space, in some form, in our brains too. A less cluttered space means a less cluttered brain and that means a brain that isn't on overload and can help deal with stress so much better.

TIP 25

When the phone rings, before answering: wait, take a breath, focus on being relaxed and calm, then answer.

Why:

Think about it, the phone never rings when we're doing nothing. Even if it appears that we're doing nothing, we are always doing something e.g. sleeping, thinking, daydreaming, emailing and things like that. But if we're with people and the phone rings we can be talking, listening or even wondering why we're not part of the crowd. So our minds are always occupied.

As I said in a couple of other tips, we can't have a thought without also having a physical sensation or an emotion. So here's the thing: if we're doing something and we're thinking about it, then we are going to have an emotion going on for us too.

Also, if you read back over Tip 22, you'll realise that multitasking is rapid switching between tasks. Now add the phone ringing into the equation. If we snatch at the phone and answer it immediately, the chances are, whatever we were doing will be disturbed and we'll take the emotion that we're feeling at that moment into our phone call.

So, if we're, for instance, feeling stressed, we will take that stress into the phone call unless we do something to break that cycle.

And one more thing. Don't people who we're talking

to deserve our full attention? I certainly think so. If we're distracted by anything else, then we won't be able to give them the respect and attention they deserve.

The next time the phone rings, don't pick it up straight away. It will keep on ringing, believe me. Take a breath (you know the deal by now – a proper breath and if you need to remind yourself how to do this, look right back to the very beginning of this book). Now focus on being calm and relaxed, and one way to do this is to say to yourself 'Calm and relaxed'. If you repeat that to yourself, your body will respond because, of course, you can't have a thought without having a physical sensation too and in order for your mind to make sense of the words 'calm' and 'relaxed' it has to manufacture that for you in some form or another, even if it's a very slight feeling. And that's good enough in this instance.

Once you've got a sense of even a touch of relaxation and calmness, then pick up the phone. Fully engage with the person you're talking to. It will make a difference, I promise!

TIP 26

Ask the right question: How can I be less stressed? = more stress; how can I be calm? = more calm.

Why:

The words we use have real resonance. We can't mention something like 'stress' without knowing, in some form, what that feels like for us.

Interestingly, even though we can often say to people, 'I know exactly how you feel', actually we can't. We can only know how *we* feel. It might be similar to the way someone else feels, but not exactly the same. And this is because we're all different. We are products of our genetics, our history and where we find ourselves right now. And that is very different from others. Even twins, although incredibly similar, also have differences.

Anyway, the important thing here is that when we talk about stress we all know what it means to us. And the moment we mention that word, our brains go searching for meaning. And then, as we can't have a thought without a physical sensation, on some, even slight, level, our bodies respond.

So, that is why it's really important to ask ourselves the right question. The moment we say what we don't want, we get it on some level.

And by the way, our brains don't respond to 'more' or 'less' before they've responded to the noun. So in order to have 'less stress' our brains and bodies have already produced 'stress' for us and only then can it start to deal with the 'more' or 'less'.

Focus on what you want. If you want to feel more calm or relaxed then be sure to tell yourself that. Then you have a good chance of your mind and body producing some calmness or relaxedness for you.

Go ahead, give it a try. No matter what I tell you, you really have to try this for yourself to see the effect it can have on your life.

TIP 27

Eating slowly leads to a calm digestive tract. Always good to start calm on the inside.

Why:
When we eat food our digestive systems kick into action straight away. We have all kinds of things going on from enzymes in our saliva that starts the process of digestion to those in our stomachs and then our intestines.

However, if we eat very fast we're not allowing for our digestions to do what they're supposed to and it can lead to all kinds of problems.

Gulping food without chewing properly starts the process off badly. It doesn't give our bodies time to get those enzymes going and consequently we not only can get digestive disorders, but also our bodies can't absorb the nutrients the food can give us. It also takes extra energy for the body to work through a 'food mass' rather than well chewed food and I'm sure I don't need to spell out what that can do!

If we eat fast, we're also at the risk of bloating and gas as we take in quite a bit of air by gulping food.

There's another bonus to eating slowly too. And that is that we feel fuller quicker as our stomach registers the food going in and we are less likely to be the victims of overeating. Apparently, it takes twenty minutes for our stomachs to recognise that food is there, so if we just throw food in we can keep on eating without realising we don't need that food.

And when we eat fast we don't get to really taste the food. Our tongues are made up of tiny taste buds that allow us to experience sweet, sour, salty and bitter, but if we don't give ourselves time to savour the taste, we're missing out.

Here's something for you to try and I'm going to give you the example of a biscuit.

The next time you reach for a biscuit, before you even put it in your mouth, look at it and then smell it. Allow your saliva to start working. Then take one small bite and chew. And, as you do so, really allow the taste to arise in your mouth. What can you taste? And once you feel you've chewed it enough (apparently the going rate is 5-10 chews for soft foods and around 30 chews for more dense or harder foods), then swallow.

Now, before you take another bite, think about this: someone went to the effort to grow the wheat that went to make the biscuit. They had to harvest it. Then they sent it off to a factory, which someone else designed and others built in order to get you this biscuit. Other ingredients, which were also grown by somebody, were added. There was a whole process going on just so you could enjoy this biscuit. So enjoy it. Oh yes, and once you've swallowed the bite of biscuit take a moment to realise that you are now one bite of biscuit heavier than you were before! Go ahead, enjoy the rest of the biscuit in the same way.

TIP 28

Goals: set 3 – bronze = totally achievable; silver = probably achievable; gold = possibly achievable.

Why:

I'm sure you've heard it a million times that goal setting is of utmost importance.

We're a goal-oriented species and setting good goals can enhance our lives significantly. I'm sure you've also heard of setting SMART goals, which are goals that are Specific, Measureable, Attainable, Relevant and Time-bound. But the thing I've found is that often, when people originally set their goals, they adhere to the formula, but then something often gets in the way of achieving those goals. And the moment the goal isn't achieved they let go of goal setting and say it doesn't work for them. I can't tell you how many times I've heard this.

I encourage anyone who comes to talk to me about setting goals to do it slightly differently.

The first thing is that SMART goals work, but then we also have to be smart with them. Instead of setting one goal I encourage people to set three. This is so that, no matter what happens or gets in the way, the goal will be achieved.

I get people to set three goals and we put them as Bronze, Silver and Gold goals.

The Bronze goal must be absolutely achievable no

matter what. The Silver goal is probably achievable and the Gold goal is possibly achievable. And I've not had anyone yet (though I know there's always a first time!) who has come back and told me this hasn't worked for them.

An example from my own life: I wanted to get a bit fitter. So I started out by saying every single day I would walk ten thousand steps. I bought myself a pedometer and stuck it on my waistband and off I went. And how long do you think that lasted? Not long I can tell you! I came down with a heavy cold and was stuck in bed for a couple of days and that put paid to that goal and I felt pretty dreadful. Ill, unfit and not achieving my goal. I changed it around and made it that my Bronze goal would be to walk up and down the stairs at least twenty times a day. This wasn't difficult even with a cold as I went up and down to the kitchen to get drinks and made sure that I was drinking lots. My Silver goal was to do five thousand steps a day, which as I began to feel better was achievable; and then my Gold goal was the ten thousand steps a day. And I have to say it worked brilliantly.

So there you have it. Don't set one goal, set three and make sure your Bronze one is totally achievable.

TIP 29

Criticism is a message wrapped up in negative packaging. Unpick the message and you could learn a lot.

Why:

Whenever we're criticised we tend to shut down or get angry or any one of those negative things that we can do. And what happens when we shut down is that we don't hear the message, which very often isn't exactly the criticism, but often something that can be very enlightening.

One of the things I teach my clients to do is to see criticism as a gift. So if you were given a gift you would accept it, say thank you for it, unwrap it and then make a decision about what you're going to do with it. So if it was a gift you liked, you'd be thinking of keeping it and what you might do with it, but if it was a gift you didn't like... well you'd maybe think about taking it to a charity shop, giving it away as a raffle prize or even throwing it in the bin! Though I have to admit there are some people who keep all the things they dislike and wonder why they feel bad about themselves, but that's another tip altogether!

What I'm trying to say is, you have choice in what you do with a gift. And actually, words are the same if we treat them as such.

If someone is being negative and criticising us we can decide what we want to do with that specific 'gift', but – and this is a big but – we have to unwrap the words first or we won't know whether it's a keeper or a throwaway. And very often when people are trying to tell us something, no matter the kind of 'packaging' it comes in, it can be very useful information.

The very next time someone criticizes you, take a pause. Notice whether you've tightened and if so, see if you can relax a bit. This is when taking a breath (and yes, if you've got this far in the tips you'll know I'm going to mention going right back to the beginning of this book and check on how to breathe to help yourself) can really help. Then think about what this person is trying to tell you. Did you do a bad job or whatever the message is?

If you did, now is the point where you have to own your mistakes. Be responsible. And then do something about it. What will you do so you don't make the same mistake again? Think creatively or, ask the person criticising how you could make it better in the future if you're not sure.

And of course, if you unwrap the message and it's of no value... don't dwell on it. Let it go. Focusing on it in these circumstances will only make you feel bad. And maybe the person was in a bad mood and just wanted to shout at someone. It happens. Not pleasant, I know, but again, if you harbour resentment all that will happen is you'll feel bad.

Make the choice. Feel good either by taking responsibility or choosing to let it go.

TIP 30

Make a list of all the things that help you feel relaxed. Do at least one of these every day this week.

Why:
When we're feeling stressed it's very difficult to think of things that relax us, so having a ready-made list can be incredibly useful.

Try and make this list while you are feeling calm and certainly when you are in a quiet place where you've got time to think.

Take out a pen and paper – this is one of those things that I think are better done the 'old fashioned' way, but if a computer is your thing, then so be it. But as you make your list think of absolutely everything, no matter how small or how big, that helps you feel relaxed.

Small things can be things like having a shower, listening to music, going for a walk; big things can be things like going to see a film, meditating, or cooking a meal for a loved one. But the main thing is to be as creative as you can be.

If you're struggling to come up with things, ask friends or family what they do to help them relax and put those on your list. And keep adding to the list whenever you come across something that you think might be relaxing.

By the time you've finished you should have quite a lot of things on there. Now put the list somewhere handy, either on a pinboard or in a drawer where you know you'll be able to locate it.

Every day this week, look at your list and pick one and do it. It doesn't matter which one you choose, and it can be the same one every day if you like. But do it.

This list isn't just for this week though, it's for life. So put it somewhere where you can see it or find it the moment you need it and, the next time you feel stressed, take a look at it and think what you could put into your life right now.

But remember, looking at the list won't help, but doing what's on the list will!

TIP 31

Chunk down. Overwhelmed with large amounts of info? Focus on one small bit at a time.

Why:

There's this great question: How do you eat an elephant? And the answer is: One bite at a time.

Or, as Henry Ford put it, 'Nothing is particularly hard if you divide it into small jobs.'

We can use this concept whenever we're overloaded and stressed because of the overwhelming amount of work or information we have to deal with. By breaking it down into small bits of work or information and focusing on just that one small bit at a time, we can get done what we need to get done, without feeling overwhelmed.

This leads to us letting go of our stressed feelings because, whenever we're accomplishing what we set out to do, we know we're getting our stuff done, but it also leads to feeling good about ourselves, which boosts our self-esteem and allows us to feel on top of things. And when we feel good about ourselves and on top of things, the things that stress us become so much easier to deal with.

TIP 32

We can learn something from everyone. It's up to us to work out what that lesson might be.

Why:
If we approach our life with the idea that everyone can teach us something we start to look outward instead of inward.

It's important to think that, no matter what a person does or says, we can learn from them.

For instance, if a person hurts us or says something mean to us, we can look at what it is they're saying or doing and make a decision on that. Or we could decide that we don't want to be like that ourselves and then can take care not to impose our negative feelings on others.

And of course, if someone does something lovely for us or says something nice, it's a whole lot easier, but then we can also make the decision to be nice to the very next person we meet, even if it's just to smile at them.

A story from my own life: when I was an assistant psychologist working in a Child and Family Department, at that time I had a supervisor who rarely used to ask me about my work or do what I'd been led to believe a supervisor was supposed to do. Instead she would tell me all about her family and how she was and how she was enjoying the job. She then left and another child psychologist took her place and the difference was incredible. He would ask me all kinds of questions – some of them not easy to answer – and I learned so much from him. I could have gone around telling everyone about how bad she was and how good he was, but instead I looked at what they both had given me and made the decision that when I was a supervisor I would make sure which one of them I took after. So you see they both taught me something – the one how not to be a supervisor and the other how to be a really good one. And I tried hard to live up to that whenever I was supervising.

Sometimes we have to look hard to find that lesson, but make no mistake, if we look for it, we'll see it.

TIP 33

If you're struggling with something, far better to ask for help than stress yourself out.

Why:
Struggling gets us nowhere. It can make us feel tight and stressed out. Here's an example: if you're trying to find your way somewhere and you don't have a satnav or a phone that's working, what happens? Well, for sure you're lost and that can lead to feelings of stress. If you ask someone for directions, you get to go where you need to be with (hopefully) minimal stress.

For some reason, many people seem to think that asking for help is a sign of weakness, but in my book it's a sign of strength.

Think about it: if you're a strong person nothing fazes you, so asking for help is just one of those things that you do sometimes. And of course, no matter what we think that's exactly how we are. So if you think you're a strong person, then that's how you'll come across. And then if you think you're a weak person... you know the answer to that one!

Also, if you ask someone for help, it can give them a good feeling to be useful. So it's a two-way thing. You get what you need sorted and the other person has an opportunity to feel useful. Let's go back to my example of losing your way: has anyone ever asked you for directions and you know exactly how they should get there? How do you feel after you've sent them on their way? Like a good, helpful person? And I'll bet the person you gave directions to was really pleased and was grateful to you for your help. When someone's grateful to you, it can engender those positive feelings.

So, look for areas in your life that you can ask for help with and see how easy it can be. And don't forget to be on the lookout for how the other person feels. Remember to say 'thank you' and watch for their reaction. See how good it feels to get your stuff sorted, but also what gratitude does for the other person.

TIP 34

If you've said something stupid, apologise. There's never a time when an apology goes amiss.

Why:
This is one of those areas where taking full responsibility for your actions is inevitably the only positive way forward. If you know you've said something stupid then carrying that around with you will only add to your stress levels and won't mend the bridges that you might have broken.

Apologising will certainly make you feel better and will, even though it may be eventual, allow the other person to feel better, or at the very least they will know you are a sincere person.

But this brings to mind one of the big no-nos when apologising and that is to apologise when you don't really mean it. The other person will know and may well feel patronized. It's a sure-fire way to make things worse.

How to apologise? The first thing you have to do is take responsibility for your actions, admit you've made a mistake and then sincerely apologise. That's it. There are some people who say you should ask for forgiveness, but I think that puts the onus on the other person. Leaving them with your sincere apology and not asking them for anything more is, in my view, sufficient. Of course you could say what you'll do in the future, but frankly a sincere apology should be enough.

When to apologise? As soon as you can. But you know what? Better late than never.

So this week look out for when you say something stupid and then apologise. Practice really does help with this and once you start you'll realise that it's a whole lot easier than you thought and certainly a whole lot better than carrying around the stressful thought that you've done something you should apologise for.

TIP 35

Are you too focused on perfection? There's no such thing as perfect. Being 'good enough' is good enough!

Why:

Perfectionism is the way to get totally stressed out and being perfect isn't a goal worth having. It's great to do our very best and to give 100% to whatever it is we're doing. But sometimes it can be easy to get carried away and try to make everything as perfect as we can.

There isn't such a thing as perfect as there are flaws in everything. No matter what it is. We can think something is wonderful, but there's always room for improvement. And that's the road to not getting things finished and feelings of stress mounting up.

I hope you can see that striving for something that doesn't exist is a bit nonsensical.

Yes, it's good to do the best you can, but then let it go. Know that if something is good enough then that's it. It's enough.

When you want something to be perfect, take a moment, stop what you're doing and breathe. I recommend two to five deep breaths (and this is where you might have to go back to the beginning of the book to remind yourself what a deep breath is like). Once you've done that, think to yourself, is this okay? Is it good enough? In my experience nine times out of ten it will be good enough. And that final tenth time I can make a few adjustments and then go through the process of taking a moment, stop what I'm doing and then take those two to five breaths again and ask myself the same questions.

TIP 36

Take time to look at what you've achieved rather than focus on all the things you wish you'd done.

Why:
Focusing on all the things we wish we'd done is a recipe for making us feel low and can really add to stress levels. Whereas if we focus on what we've achieved it can make us feel positive and can be a motivator.

Achievements, no matter how small, are achievements. Simple as that.

If you're trying to get something finished and you're struggling, stop for a moment and look at what you've already done. Pat yourself on the back and feel proud. Again, it doesn't matter if what you've achieved is just small. It's still deserving of positivity and can spur you on to achieve a little more.

Here's one from my own life: when I was writing this book, I was a little disappointed that in my first week I'd only written approximately 7,000 words. But luckily I had a buddy, who was working on her book at the same time, who reminded me that it was 7,000 words more than I had the week before. I know this sounds obvious, but we often don't think about it in that way, especially when we're focused on the end product. It gave me huge incentive to keep writing.

If you're truly stuck then take a break, but only after

you've looked at what you've done and given yourself some positive strokes. Do something different, like stretching or a relaxation exercise, and then get back to what you need to do.

TIP 37

When feeling stressed ask yourself, 'What would I say to a friend?' Listen to your own wise words.

Why:
We can often find ourselves bad mouthing ourselves in our heads. What's worse is telling ourselves that we're stressed and not coping, because the moment we focus on stress that's exactly what we get.

But if a friend was stressed and being hard on themselves, what would you say to them? None of us would tell them they're a dreadful person and that they deserve to feel stressed. Instead, you would listen to them and be supportive and maybe give them some ideas of how to relax and to move away from those stressy feelings. But it's funny how often we do the opposite with ourselves.

If you're feeling stressed, stop for a moment and take a breath (yes, that is that deep breath that you'll find the instructions for at the beginning of this book!) and then ask yourself, 'What would I say to a friend in this situation?' And then pay attention to your own wise words and take action on them.

TIP 38

Procrastination increases stress. If we leave things they just build up in our minds. Do it now!

Why:

Whenever we procrastinate, what do you think happens? Do you think you forget about the job in hand? Of course you don't! What happens is that the job is still in the mind taking up energy and reminding us over and over that it still needs to get done. And that just leads to increased stress.

The more you procrastinate, the more you're setting yourself up for adding to your stress levels.

Stop procrastinating and get the job done now! You can even combine it with the tip from Week 38 and congratulate yourself with each small step that you take in completing the task that you need to get on with. And before you realise it, the job will be done and dusted. And you'll feel so much better for it.

TIP 39

Do you wish you were appreciated more? It starts with us. Show others they're appreciated.

Why:
Whenever we want something, such as to be appreciated more, it's funny how we almost demand that others do it to us first. We want to know that they appreciate us. And we want them to show it. But the thing is, if we don't show others that we appreciate them, how on earth can we expect others to show us we're appreciated? It always has to start with us.

We need to model for those around us how we want them to behave with us and lead by example. Only then can we expect others to know what to do.

The same goes for those we love. Do we tell them, or do we just think that they know we love them? Think when you were last told you were loved and appreciated. How did it make you feel? And what did it make you feel like doing? Hopefully reciprocate, by showing that person that you love and appreciate them too.

Remember this week to show everyone how much you appreciate them, even for the very small things that they do. It only has to be a 'thank you' when someone opens a door for you, for instance, or keeps the elevator door open so you can get in, or when you're cooked a dinner. I'm sure you can come up with loads of situations where you can practise appreciating others.

Once you start appreciating it's amazing how people then start to appreciate you.

Remember, it always starts with us.

TIP 40

When feeling stressed, take a breath and smile. Smiling can change your state of mind just like that.

Why:
We can't be stressed and relaxed/happy at the same time. It's just not possible. And whenever we have an emotion or feeling, we also have a physical sensation and a thought (or many) that go with that emotion or feeling.

A very simple way of changing your state is to change what you do. And smiling is one of those incredibly simple things that takes very little to do, but can change a whole lot about how you feel and the thoughts that you have.

Try for one moment to bring to mind something or somebody that makes you smile. It can be anything at all. The smile only has to be slight. Notice what happens to the rest of your body as you do this. What thoughts are in your mind as you think about this person or thing that brings a smile to your face? Now, keep that smile there and try to think of something stressful. Not easy, eh? The moment you do think of something stressful, what's happened to your mouth? Has it tightened away from a smile? Now think of that person or thing that makes you smile again. Notice the difference?

We literally can't hold both of those things together at the same time and there's always a choice to bring to mind something that makes us smile if we choose to. It really is a matter of choice. So what do you want to be, tight and stressed or smiling and relaxed?

TIP 41

Do you often tell yourself you can't? Remind yourself you can, you just need to find out how.

Why:
First off, whatever we tell ourselves is absolutely true. As Henry Ford said, 'Whether you think you can, or you think you can't – you're right'. So we have to be very careful what we say to ourselves.

But the thing is, very often we say we can't when actually we mean that we don't have the wherewithal right this moment to know how to move from the stage of 'can't' to the stage of 'can'. So we get stuck with 'I can't' and get frustrated, angry or depressed and stressed with ourselves.

Think about it though. There's quite a big difference in telling yourself, 'I can't' to telling yourself, 'I don't know how'. One is categorical and feels stuck whereas the other has kind of movement to it. Or to put it another way, 'I can't' is definitive in and of itself, 'I don't know how' suggests that there is a way forward, just that you don't, at this point in time, know exactly what that way forward is.

If you don't know how to do something, there's no point being harsh and critical. What we don't know, we don't know! But we can ask ourselves, 'How could I find out?' And now there's some freedom, because, for instance, we can ask someone for help, we can look stuff up, we can go on Google and search or even go on Facebook and ask our friends what they would do. So many different ways and approaches that will lead to the possibility of an 'I can'.

The very next time you hear yourself saying to others or in your head, 'I can't' remind yourself that you can, you just need to find out how. And if you hear someone else saying, 'I can't' you could perhaps offer to help them. Nothing like helping someone else to help you feel good about yourself.

TIP 42

What else is going on in your world apart from feeling stressed? Notice the what else and focus on that.

Why:
When we're stressed we look at the world a certain way. We actually look for all the things that are stressing us out and what happens then is that it becomes cyclical. We are stressed, we look for stressy things and that makes us more stressed and on and on it goes until we feel consumed by stress and totally overwhelmed.

But that's not all that's happening in our world. There are loads of other things, but we just can't see them because we're not looking for them. And what we look for is what we get. Look for stress and we'll see stress, look for things that make us feel calm and relaxed and that's what we'll see.

The trick is to widen our awareness so we can be open to the other things that are going on and this is how I suggest people do it.

Start by stopping and taking a breath or two (and yes, time to go back to the beginning of the book and check that you've got your breathing right). Now, say to yourself, 'What can I see around me that makes me feel calm and relaxed?' Think about those words 'calm' and 'relaxed'. Notice what's happening in your body and if you notice tension, just think about where that tension is and again say, 'calm' and 'relaxed'. Do this until you feel the tension easing. How do you feel now? The stressed feelings should have dissipated. If not, start again by taking a breath and repeat the instructions until the stressed feelings dissipate.

And then we can look at the world from a calm and relaxed point of view.

It doesn't mean that the stress has gone, but it does give a chance to realise that we don't have to get stuck in stress, we can move ourselves away from those feelings quite easily if we choose to.

TIP 43

How often are you kind to yourself? Take a moment each day and focus on doing just that.

Why:
Do you ever listen to the tone of voice you use to yourself in your head? Is it kind? Most people say that what they hear is usually a critical voice that tells them over and over, in very negative terms, negative things about themselves.

If we talk to ourselves negatively it can be a real downer and if we're stressed and we tell ourselves continually that we're stupid or we can't do such and such, it's certainly not going to get rid of our stress, but add far more to it. Because, of course, what we tell ourselves we believe, even if it's just minimally (though I would contend that we tend to maximise not minimise) and once there's a glimmer of telling ourselves we're stressed, what we become is stressed. This is because we can't hold a thought in our heads and not react to it on some level.

This week, whenever you hear yourself being unkind or critical, stop and change the voice to being one of supportiveness.

Also, every single day, spend a moment being kind to yourself. A very good time to do this is either first thing in the morning or last thing at night – or preferably both!

TIP 44

Got lots to do? Try doing the hardest thing first.

Why:

Have you ever noticed how when you have lots of tasks to complete that you complete the easy ones first and leave the hardest one until the end? And this often means that the hardest one is not completed, but left on the 'to do' list waiting for the next time, and then the same thing happens.

If we do things this way round, the hardest thing is still on our minds all the time while we're completing the easy tasks. It's like a portion of our brain is taken up knowing it's waiting in the wings and this can add significantly to our stress levels.

It's very tempting to get on with the easy things, just because they're easy. But if we complete the hardest one first, it's no longer bugging us, or taking up brain energy. Not only is it a relief that it's done, it can add to a sense of feeling good at having completed it and also allows us to let go of the stress attached to it.

So this week try doing the hardest task on your 'to do' list first and see how positive it can let you feel.

TIP 45

Have problems when someone compliments you? A simple 'thank you' will do.

Why:

When someone compliments you, what do you do? Do you just say 'thank you' or do you go into a 'oh, this old thing' kind of mode where it's almost as if you're making excuses for receiving the compliment. So, in a funny way, receiving a compliment can add to stress levels.

Think of a compliment as though it were a gift – which of course it is. When someone gives us a gift the first thing that comes to our minds is gratitude. We say 'thank you' and maybe 'that's kind', but we don't go into huge explanations as to why we're grateful, it's just that we are. And if we treat a compliment in exactly the same way it can free us from all that nonsense of excuse making.

Excuse making implies we don't deserve the compliment. Nevertheless, it's been given and the giving, in and of itself, deserves our thanks.

However, this takes practice. The first time you try to stop yourself at 'thank you' I'm sure you'll think you should be adding to it and it can feel a bit difficult not doing so. But once you get into this it's very simple, there's no self-deprecation going on and it can make the other person feel as though you've got what they were trying to say.

Self-deprecation only makes the other person, the one who gives the compliment, feel negative about giving compliments.

All you need is a simple 'thank you'.

TIP 46

'Act as if' – when you feel stressed see if you can act as if you are calm and relaxed.

Why:
When we're stressed we act a certain way and when we're calm we act a very different way. You can change how you feel when you're stressed by acting as if you're feeling calm.

Think about your body when it's calm and relaxed. How do you stand or sit? Now see if you can stand or sit like that right now.

What you'll need to do is to think about what the calm you looks like. Do you relax your shoulders? Your arms? Your hands? What happens to your face when you're calm and relaxed? Fully immerse yourself in how you think you are. Now, what happens when you walk about? See if you can maintain that body posture as you move. Then think about talking in a relaxed and calm way. Has your breathing altered? If not, remember you can always dip back to the beginning of this book and revisit the paragraphs on deep, calm breathing and then do it right now.

So the next time you notice stress arising, remember you can always choose to act calm and relaxed. It really helps.

TIP 47

Fear of failure? Think about it: failure is just feedback. Use it wisely.

Why:

Baudjuin said, 'No matter how hard you work for success, if your thought is saturated with fear of failure it will kill your efforts, neutralize your endeavours and make success impossible.'

Fear of failure can often stop us from achieving what we want. Instead of thinking of it as something negative, if we think about failure as feedback it can be very positive to fail. All it really means is that we haven't found the right way to do whatever it is we're doing.

Did you know that some of the most famous inventions would never have been made if the inventors had stopped at their first failure? For instance, Thomas Edison, inventor of the light bulb had 1,000 failed attempts at creating one light bulb that worked properly. When he was asked how it felt to fail 1,000 times Edison answered, 'I didn't fail 1,000 times. The light bulb was an invention of 1,000 steps.' Or as Henry Ford said, 'Failure provides the opportunity to begin again, more intelligently,' and don't forget that Henry Ford failed and went broke five times before he succeeded. And Bobby Jones, the famous American golfer said, 'I never learned anything from a tournament I won.'

The next time you feel scared to even try because

you're frightened of failing, remember that not getting something right is okay as long as you use that information to correct, and keep correcting, until you achieve what you want.

So fail away, but learn from your mistakes and try again armed with information about how not to do whatever it is you're doing and keep going until you get it right.

TIP 48

Thinking about things doesn't get them done.

Why:
We can spend a lot of our time thinking about what we should be doing, or could be doing. Sadly, when we sit and think it's not actually getting tasks done.

Of course, we do need thinking time, but there are times to think and times to do. And it's important to know the difference.

When we're planning something or problem solving then thinking time is very important and doing can be a distraction from this working things out. But when it's time for action it's amazing how we can sit and spend an inordinate amount of time thinking, when actually we just need to get on and do the tasks.

The other point I'd like to make is about when our thoughts become things to beat ourselves up with. The moment we hear ourselves saying things like 'I could', or 'I would', or 'I should' or 'I ought' we need to take great care. These words are ones that keep us in the thinking loop and are about past or about future, but not about the right now and are guaranteed to make sure we stay stuck in not getting on with tasks in hand and feeling bad about ourselves at the same time. Essentially they're criticisms. Or as I like to put it, 'Coulda, woulda, shoulda' never achieves anything.

Be on the lookout this week for when you're thinking

and not doing. When you should be getting on with things, remind yourself to get on with your task right now.

TIP 49

Instead of saying 'I have to' try saying 'I get to'. It makes a big difference. Very empowering.

Why:
Whenever we tell ourselves we have to do something, it implies we have no choice in the matter and it also has a 'heavy' feel about it. And this can lead to us feeling more stressed. However, by changing the 'I have to' to 'I get to' it alters the whole feel.

Think about it. Take a simple sentence like, 'I have to get up'. Say it to yourself. How does it make you feel? Now, change it to, 'I get to get up.' What happens? Well it implies freedom and that you have choice and that it's exciting.

When we get to do something, we're telling ourselves that we're lucky. And of course there are some people who can't get up, so we are very lucky to be able to do so. But more than that, when we have choice and we don't feel the constraints put on us by someone else it lessens our feelings of stress and, what's more, adds a sense of lightness.

This week, watch out for every time you say 'I have to...' and change it to 'I get to...' and feel how empowering it is.

TIP 50

Focus on being calm, then see if you can spread it beyond you to 'infect' those around you.

Why:
This is one of my absolute favourites and something I often task people with who are prone to feeling stressed.

Feelings are very easy to pick up on, and the more negative feelings are the easiest. When someone comes into a room and they're in a bad mood they don't even have to say anything, we automatically know their mood. This is because of the energy they give off. Equally, when someone enters in a great mood, we also know.

We're always giving off energy, because we're made of energy.

But the thing is, although negative energy is very easy to pick up on, we can change the negative energy by giving out as much positive energy as possible. Or as I like to say, we can 'infect' people with calm.

When we are stressed, it's extremely easy to spread that stress so that others start to feel stressed too. What I encourage people to do is to calm themselves down by using any of the tips in this book that have helped, then imagine that calmness spreading from themselves and seeing how quickly they can effect calmness in others.

The kind of things to say in the mind at this point are things like, 'How quickly can I spread calmness from myself to others,' or 'I'm spreading the calmness from myself to everyone else around me.'

One brilliant way of using this, I've found, is in airports. Usually they are quite stressful places, especially when people are queuing at the check-in desk. Whenever I'm in the queue, I quieten my mind, think about calm and relaxation and then see how quickly I can get the people around me to be calm and relaxed. And it works! I've managed to see people who were all antsy and frowning to calm down and then talk to me all happy and calm.

This tip works on so many levels. From the way you calm yourself down, to managing to calm a whole space full of people. And if you have children who are a bit hyper, try sitting and breathing and thinking calmness and relaxation. It might take a moment or two, but I've found they calm down pretty quick.

And the thing is, it's such a lovely thing to do. It's like giving people a gift, but they're not sure where it's coming from. Rather like an anonymous gift. Knowing you're doing something positive not just for yourself, but for others too.

I really hope you try this out.

BONUS TIPS

CHRISTMAS TIP

Make absolutely sure you have some 'me' time.

Why:
Christmas can be a really stressful time. If we're continually looking after everyone else, trying to make it a good time for all and sundry and not giving ourselves a break, it's very easy to become angry and critical, tense and stressed out.

Take a bit of time out and do something that pleases you and then come back into the 'fray' feeling refreshed and calm.

Anything that helps you to calm down and smile is the thing to go for, even if it's something simple like a shower, or putting your headphones on and listening to your favourite music or something more complex like listening to a relaxation tape or meditating. It doesn't matter what it is as long as it does the trick.

NEW YEAR TIP

Think of all the people you've done something for over the last year and congratulate yourself and SMILE.

Why:

It can be very easy to get caught up in self-criticism, especially at this time of the year when we turn towards the future, often making resolutions about the things we haven't done and feel like we should be achieving.

But if we can think about others and what we've done for them, it can really help to feel good about ourselves. It doesn't matter how small a thing you might have done. It can be something simple like smiling at someone in the street, or opening a door for someone, to something more complex like helping someone out.

Go on. Think of all those things. Every single one. Go back to January 1st last year and think. Did you do anything for anyone? Made someone a cup of tea? Did you buy someone a drink? Give someone a compliment? Phoned a friend and listened to them? And what about when you were at work – did you at least once this year work well? Because if you think about it, when you work well it helps the company you work for and helps pay someone's wages. Really broaden your thinking to encompass all those small things that could go unnoticed and all those big things that make you feel proud to be you.

The next part of the task is to smile. Go back to Week 42 and read up on that tip to remind yourself about the power of smiling.

It's a great way to start the New Year

ABOUT THE AUTHOR

Dr Vee Freir is a seven-eighths retired Consultant Clinical Psychologist who has worked in both the Scottish NHS and the private sector. She has worked with children, young people and families, in cancer care and in adult mental health.

Dr Vee wrote a pocket book called START To Stress Less in 2008, which is a five-step programme to overcoming stress. After writing that book she started writing a weekly tip of the week on Twitter that culminated in this book.

She currently teaches Mindfulness and Qiqong (a form of exercise akin to T'ai Chi) at various places around the world. And she also does one-to-one stress management sessions.

Dr Vee is also a published poet.

PLEASE LEAVE FEEDBACK!

Thank you for reading this book. I'd really appreciate any feedback and would love to hear what you have to say.

Please leave a helpful review on Amazon.

Thank you!

Vee

Made in the USA
Charleston, SC
06 July 2016